Unfinished Suite:

Poetry & Prose

Mark C. LLoyd

No Frills
<<<>>>
Buffalo
Buffalo, NY

Printed in the United States of America

LLoyd, Mark C.

Unfinished Suite: Poetry & Prose/LLoyd- 1st Edition

ISBN: 978-0-0-9896220-1-1

1. Unfinished Suite - Poetry- Prose   2. New Author – No Frills. 3. Poetry. 4. Prose
1. Title

No Frills Buffalo Press
119 Dorchester Buffalo, New York 14213
For More Information Visit Nofrillsbuffalo.co

The appreciations:

My Parents, my family, my friends, Fred, Nikki, Julie and
Tracy ...
and my little Boo-Boo. Some have passed and my heart is
missing you.

To all the people who just don't get me:

All Writers need friends and support ... I love and
appreciate those who support me ... but sometimes it's
those people who don't support me who make me Write
more ... and make me better.

"Unfinished Suite"

I've a Poet's voice with a Comedian's face
I can see in your eyes I'm not what you expected
I'm the tragic Shakespearean sonnet that's not
perfected
I'll never be that Claude Debussy suite
Clair de lune on the piano
A Claude Monet painting in Venice
I am Quasimodo of words
An Emmett Kelly behind some oil and grease
I'm that unfinished suite that an artist never
completes

- Mark C. LLoyd, 2012

Wine, Cigarettes, Poetry, and that Red Hair

"4 a.m."

At 4 a.m.
I'm awake for you

With the terror
sometimes
the tears that it's accompanied by

It was at 4 a.m. that we would
sometimes
have our most important
conversations

As I would sit numb
half asleep
I would try to relax your confusions

At this crazy hour
of 4 a.m.
Your presence
only a spirit of our past
I still speak to you
And this is sometimes
still
my day's
most important
conversation

"If Only Life"

I remember the warmth of your body
On a cold Autumn evening
Sitting next to you in the dark theater
We watched Gere and Ryder
I could feel a life start
You smiling wide
Emotions I cannot remember having for years
Your thin fingers holding my almost bear claw hand
The coming attractions ended
Then the feature began
A hand squeeze from me drops your head onto my shoulder
The movie dialogue rolls
We are lost
In the movie fantasy of now
Life's reality ended for two hours
A few popcorn tossings later
The lights rise
We step into the misty rain of October
The aroma of Saturday night restaurants shift smoothly
We breathe in
the moment
It is still
So calm
If only life stayed this way
Like a dark theater
Full of calm fantasy

"Near the Window"

She drinks alone
in the moon glow
of 3 a.m.

A ribbon of smoke rings
silhouette her frame
as the cigarette burns

She listens
near the window

The raindrops
splashing hard puddles
in the outside flower boxes

"A Seasoned Woman"

A seasoned girl
aloof in her world
filled of fantasy and missing moments
Rough around the edges
and the bitter reality of fear
Dark moments of mistrust
mixed with the truth
make for deep anger of misunderstanding
and the inner sweetness and superficial aloofness
Which makes
for a seasoned
woman

"The Breeze Is Like Kisses from Angels"

As I sit here on my favorite bench
It's the bench where I come to speak to you
sometimes the coffee keeps me warm
an occasional cigar to push my blood pressure
to its limit
But I speak to you nonetheless
The tourists annoy me
they take photos of the Falls
and chatter
I don't like the fucking chatter
I breathe in mouthfuls of smoke
Push it out in a gust
I watch it swirl away from my face and over
my head
I can almost see your profile
Then the breeze kicks in and brushes my face
You are here then gone
The breeze is like kisses from angels on my cheek

"A Life"

Four years ago I had a
different life
I had a life of
chaos and some confusion
But now
four years later
That part of me is gone
and I wish back the chaos
and all the confusion
and I wish back you

"These Words"

Yes
You are alone
in your apartment
Your own boulevard of broken dreams and wishes
You sit alone
cigarette in one hand
and wine in the other
I can see you still
waiting for this life to open up
make some hell disappear
that fresh hell that Dottie Parker used to speak of
You sit alone and write
your mind races faster than your tiny thin Barbie doll
fingers
can type
the cigarettes never falter
they burn and glow all night
And like a pub in Ireland
the wine never lessens
and you sip until you can see no more
but still you write
You sit alone
with broken dreams
half empty passions
and still find a way to put feelings down
with the slamming on the smoky discolored keys

You cry
get angry
then start again tomorrow
These words tonight

that I read
may not be yours
but my words
pretty poet
are never without you

"Before The Darkness Comes"

Sometimes anger is confused with grief
A thief named grief can take
Confuse
Toy
Destroy
Make unlimited minutes of heartache
Remove the innocence
Of any person
From even the most naïve of people
That thief known as grief has taken that from me
My innocence is gone
It will forever be lost
The shadow of me is different
And each time
before the darkness comes
the shivers I feel
grief tries to control and take over my mind
I fight and normally win
But winning records are made to be broken
That thief named grief still side swipes me
Hits me hard
No thirty day notice
This thief steals now
It can happen
In a park
at a movie
Or in bed
Alone
The thief is always there
It wants to control
And at times
before the darkness comes

I think of you
You are my grief
You caused this darkness
The almost
Uncontrollable
thief
named grief
that enters my mind
And then when it's there
All ready to steal from me
you come back with a memory
The memory that saves me
And takes this thief named grief away
You always seem to be there
With a memory
Before the darkness comes

"Empty Space"

I watch your empty space
Breathe in the aroma of distant perfume
feel the warmth where you once laid
The empty space is full
memories
sincerity
I touch the unseen splendor
close my eyes to kiss the apparition
I watch your space
it becomes a part of mine
it always was
we shared
what was and wasn't there
and what is and isn't here
So, why wouldn't we share the empty space we leave
behind

I only wish you were filling it now...

"I Miss You In The Rain"

I miss you in the rain
when you sit on that park bench
a cool fall evening's mist hits your cat-like glasses
your tiny frame

I miss you in the rain as I now sit there alone
waiting for your full laugh and puffy crying eyes

Waiting for someone to return
who can't

I miss you in the rain

I miss you
in the Spring
in the Summer
in the Winter
in the Fall

I miss you in the Rain

I miss you in the Rain

"I Received Your Pain"

I still get heartbroken
when
I think of you
You were one of the very few who understood me
Even if you could never understand yourself
You accepted me "as is"
The eccentricities
The aloofness
The coldness
And for all that
you received
part
of my heart
all of my soul
I received your pain
when you left this world
I still get heartbroken when
I think of you
I get the late night chills
The early morning numbness

And when the sun wakes after me
it brings relief
but only because the darkness has left for a few hours
You received my soul

It's the most precious gift I could give to you
But it was a good trade
Painful as it can be at times
It was a good trade
You grabbed my soul
A part of my heart

Never let them go
I still have my heart
I know this
I get heartbroken when I think of you

"This Room Keeps Telling Me You're Not Coming Back"

It's been three days since you died
and this room keeps telling me
You're not coming back
The lonely desk
and it's uncomfortable
oversized chair
You felt like Alice
in her wonderland
My sweet poet
your old wonderland is now forever
lost to me
But this room still speaks
sometimes too loud to listen
I can still smell your perfume
and Thursday nights wine and cigarettes
and hear yesterday's voice
You speak in whispers
and in laughs
This room is too full of memories
and memories can be cruel
And at times your laugh
poetic charms
push away my fears
But this cruel room
still speaks
And it keeps telling me
You're not coming back

"Away from You"

It's been too many years
Eight and a half
Heartache doesn't get easier
It only gets more tolerable
The cracks in my heart
the wrinkles on my smile
are
from you
You have aged me
The tears don't dry with time
They only become more predictable
I don't miss you any less
I walk slower
My steps are not as solid as they used to be
My heart does age faster
It's cracks can't be filled with anything other than
the loneliness you left there
I hope any pain you felt
while alive
Is
gone
And it's the pain I feel now
Without you
Away from you
It's the heartache I was given
It's the tradeoff of your heart to mine
To remove all the pain
take it
Away from you

"Your Last Gasp"

I watched your last gasp
I watched as your thirty-two year old soul escaped from
your body and all I had was the beauty cradled in my arms
Your last gasp took away years from me
These are years I'll never get back
but they are years I don't want
I watched your last gasp as death stole a precious gift
Your soul left early one morning several years ago
I watched your last gasp
You wake me from my dreams when it's too dark
To think
with my own gasp of breath
I wake and sleep to see you leave this world
I could feel you slowly leave with that gasp of breath
I watched your last
gasp as it
stole my soul

"Strange Angel"

Strange angel
Dancing in my dreams
You have completed your needs
he needs to be seen
The want to be heard
Now
strange angel
You control my cry
live, create and clutter my mind
Write with our tears
Strange angel
And when I feel the need to stop
can't breath
without you
when the wind moves
I can feel the breeze from your lips
as you kiss my cheek
I know it'll be you
Then with eyes shut
I will see you smile
so clear
You smile
Dear strange angel
keep the wind moving
keep me breathing
Until we complete our dreams

"Muse"

The red hair bobs down
sleeps on your cheek
as a tear strolls down that classic face
to drop
on such a gentle cloud
The poet of my dreams
the muse of my life
I couldn't live with you
but I certainly
find it even more difficult
to live
without you

"I Remember So Much"

The memories of past relationships are sometimes the
hardest for us
The coldness we had
The thoughtless decisions
The hurt
We put all this behind us and move onto the other
mistakes of our life
We hope to grow
The person I was fifteen years ago is different from
today
Good and Bad
I've dealt with love
Horrible grief
I've had some beautiful moments as well
The heartbreak still hurts
Love for me never ends
It may fade a little from time to time
Then hits me at any second of the day
But the same can be said of happiness
I've had plenty
I've laughed more than many
Being eccentric does have its perks
Memories are fantastic
Memories can be cruel
I laugh and cry at mine
I guess that's the way life should be or is
Memories
I remember so much

"This Moment"

In the crisp dusk of the 990
with a sharp breeze that cut
this reddish leaf
flies into my window
hits my lips

Its as red as
your hair
and taste of maple, love and autumn

I can feel its veins
as if your fingertips
were pressing

And for this very brief moment
you are with me
in this fantasy
and I feel safe

"Warm Blooded Mornings"

I see the red in your hair
the Irish of your skin
I see the black of your lashes hug
your blue and green marbled eyes

I see your petite frame dressed
in your classic style

I see the hair elevated above
those tiny shoulders
but still on a fallen cloud

I see that hesitant smile
on that impulsive woman
on those warm blooded mornings

MERCURIAL POET

"Dream When We Need To"

Dream when you need to
Rising glow
Falling shade
And you'll find the memories
They are
ones
That no one else will
believe
it could be true
all a lie
distorted by love
time
you stood there
in the dream
Waiting for
Sun
to rise
And the Moon
Leaves
Your dancing shadow on my lips
Whispers of your love
My sweat is your soul
My eyes have
All your tears
you dream
when I need to
It's never lost
Dream when we need to

"Reality"

With your back toward me
I watch you sit
in that way that makes
a man's mind juices shift
in that way a woman can
do so well

I watch your coal black hair
rest on your sleek collar
Your shoulders shift with each new thought
 with each new emotion

You fill the tiny chair
your jean covered legs cross
a tango dancer in motion

Finger tips beating at your laptop
lively cheeks push your
drooped glasses away from the
end of that sensual nose
And when your cell phone rings
a splatter of now
tossed into my world

You whisper a smile to the caller
My thoughts come back to
... Reality

"I Want To Make Snow Angels with You"

I want to make snow angels with you
See you swooshing your arms like a bird
You
Giggle
I want to grab
Hug you
Pick you up
Your tiny self
As I hold you
You get angry
You laugh
I want to make snow angels with you
I want to be ten years old
Again
I want to see the cold steam come
from our kisses
Snow angels
We fall together
You on top
I brace you from the falling hurt
No pain
For me
Could ever
get past your laugh
I want to make snow angels tonight
In the cold
The frigid dark
My lips are cold
My tears are warm
I feel your mittens on my ears
Your nose against mine

We roll
Snow in your collar
Then the cold laughing scream
Snow angels tonight
Flap
Swoosh
Now
Tonight
The Moon watches
We're not alone
Clouds dance the dance of snow and winter
You
Make it feel like
Spring
Make me laugh
One more tickle
A roaring giggle
Roll on top
The clouds cover the moons eyes
The vapors dance around your red lips
So long have I waited for this kiss
Bury yourself in my warmth
My chest is your pillow
I want to make snow angels with
Only you

"Memories Of A Sunday"

Pieces of flowers
the chorus bell is ringing
Something about a bell
Ringing
makes me numb
brings back memories from a church
It makes me think of Sundays and Christmas
I don't remember all the Summers, Springs and
Autumns and sunny days

... but I do remember the Sunday mornings

"I Want to Watch You Dance in the Bubbles on the Corner"

I want to watch you dance in the bubbles on the
corner
On the second day of summer
On a searing summer night
... Sweaty glossy ebony skin
Summer dress, bare feet and bubbles
dancing
on the corner
in the wind

"Last Night I Thought"

Last night I thought
that Wine
would make us smile
together

Last night I thought
that Art would make us speak
together

Last night
I just thought
too much

"Insignificant"

That's the way you made me feel
Ignored
Uninterested
No reply
Gentle sighs
Seldom a "Hi"
Insignificant
That's the way you made me feel
Feelings of always a lonely "Good-bye"
Be there?
Not there
Giving
Seldom getting
In sig nif
I
cant
That's the way you made me feel

"My Immortality Has Lost Its Life"

I'm out of sync
Out of bounds
I've crossed the line
Crossed my heart
Failed to care
My immortality has lost its life
I find it rich
To live a bitch
A life
Has always been
Out of sync
My choice
Not always
Is
Now
Was is gone
Will be here
Cross my heart
Hope to die
Out of sync
Its mortality we fear with life
fear
Immortality
Without life
Is out of sync
And a hell of a fucking ride

"The Wilted Flower"

I placed
the flower
that's really a weed
on your keyboard
The yellow weed
they call the Dandelion
It lays slowly wilting
away from us

The smile
You show me
for only a brief moment

The smile that I will
put to memory
until I think no more
Is worth this moment
in life
you gave me

"This Simple Act"

The simple act
of a Dad
and his Daughter
walking a puppy
on an early Saturday morning
The carefree pup
a drama filled teen
She wishes she were prettier
and the teacher would like her

The simple act
of this cold November walk
He listens and is confused
he speaks
And like the pup
is easily distracted
She tells of her week
And the cold air becomes sentences
They stop
watch a squirrel as it climbs a tree
They laugh
as the pup bounces from its leash at the furry gray
entertainment

This simple act
she holds her Dad's icy hand
calls the pups name
And they walk
And this simple act
of morning distractions
and the chilly vapors of her week

on this early frigid Saturday morning
continues
as they cross the street

"Dandelions in the Park"

Two elderly women
holding hands
picking Dandelions in the park
Nothing on their minds
but guiding each other
and picking Dandelions in the park
Hands that have aged
faces with creases
Dreams that have left them
sleep that will take them
Heels that are too high
perfume that is too strong
Faded eyes
blotted out by faded glasses
Crooked ole smile
to go with the crooked ole walk
Superficial wishes
and superficial scenes
Reaching down
to pick
a Dandelion
in the park.

"This Song Brings Back Memories"

This song brings back memories
from a year ago
before I met you
when beauty was just superficial
and now
to be inside you
the way you shiver
shake
laugh
the way you taste when you're aroused
the way you make me sweat by just touching me
This song brings back memories of how I never really
knew how it felt
to be inside you
your knees
rubbing on my hips
squeezing
bucking
being inside you
it's not superficial
This song
Memories
The way my forehead would drip
Onto
Your breast
Leaving a ribbon of my passion rolling down and in
between
And today
This song
Leaves a memory
Of being inside you

"Willow"

Who is not here to feed the falling?
Feel the trembling
Push away the tickling grasp of vulnerability
Latch onto the emotion and push away the fear

The eagle dares to push away the wind

Run wild
Fly wild
Go fast

Spring past the darken
into another's grasp

A willow cries in the wind

"Slips Away"

He sits and watches his life
slip away

A chicken wing stained
white shirt
yellow tipped fingers
from a pack a day habit

He watches his life
slip away

"Allen Street"

Black and White
Nietzsche's
Her skirt is too tight
I don't mind
Books on the sidewalk
This one came out in the 1970's
and only a quarter
Why does a John Steinbeck look so new and unread?
but Nora Roberts look so worn?
Record albums existed before CD's
They were round
had grooves
scratched easily
could actually melt
you couldn't play them in your car
but when the album sucked
they made great Frisbees in the park
and the covers used to fade
College street Gallery
Allen Street Hardware
Soup
Martinis
Potted flowers
This brunette
her hair is curly and looks wet
wears a dress shirt
She's got back

but her fronts nice
The man with the frayed bottom jeans
The trees move slowly
Why is that hair look so much younger than his face

She reads a poem
These two guys
don't listen
the alcohol makes their minds mush
That old lady
her eyes are watery
her mouth is dry and she bums a cigarette
she shakes
trembles
could be crack
could be booze
could be that her mind gave out too soon

but she's listening

"Elmwood"

I'm eating on Elmwood
      Not on the street
In a restaurant
Does it matter which one?
      No
      Not important
It's still the Avenue
I can smell Elmwood
      The aroma of
      Burnt toast
      And bagels
Coffee brewed and brewing
Elmwood
smells like tomorrow if it were perfect

"...or do we?"

Do I forget
go on
I never stopped either
or do I just think about it
Do I try and smile when
I think of you
or do I cry
Do I wake up and get out of bed
or stay in bed and give up for that day
Do I think of you and all the good times
or just the bad ones
to make it easier
Do I really have anything to give
or should I just
give in
give out
give up
Do I forget
go on
Does love ever end
or does it just change
Do we
Should we
Love doesn't end
sometimes
we do
or do we?

Women and the art of Women ... for every woman who broke my heart, for every woman I didn't meet but I wanted to ...

"She Exhales in the Rain"

High heels
short skirts
and the silk that clings

You smoke
a cigarette
in the rain

As fog rises
from sewer vents
you make those last passionate puffs

Full lips pursed
a very lipstick red

No smoking
Inside
for the inhaling

Looking through
the steamed covered
smoke screens

They look from inside
out

You stand
and bounce
as your cat-like glasses
grow a foggy mist

Cold knees
angry ego
and the mist from
sidewalk vents
surround those heels

As you exhale
In
the
rain

"... your heels on the wooden floor in the dark"

All I could hear were your heel clicks on
that wooden floor
It was that sensual dance that stirred in my mind
Emotions that tossed away my inhibitions
That covered up the love that can make a man cry
I could imagine your hip swaying
Like the Femme fatale you always envisioned yourself
as
The kind that controls a man with a smile
clicks their high heels on rain wet cement
In the darkness of the room
Only the light from the street
I could see your curvy, tiny frame
Red hair pushing through
The cigarette smoke making brush strokes
around your face and white streams of light that
silhouette you and bounce
off the wall and floors and the lovely sound
of your heels
on the wooden floor
in the dark
Nothing could beat the lovely sound
of your heels
on the wooden floor
in the dark

"...With Every Smile"

You cry at every smile
It does not hide the fear inside the body of proud
sarcasm
Anger shows a woman in hurt
Your pain is sometimes well-hidden
deep into the body like a cocoon living to come out
A gland is only slightly moistened
A fluttering shaped tear hits the cheek
Are you crying for the moment or for the past?
A past you never deny
You never forget
Always defy
You smile out and cry
Always honest
Always direct
Eyes looked to forget
A panic sets in when it is discovered
A woman who is looking inside
To find a girl who was hurt and felt rejected
If only a single tear could wash away that pain . . .
I'd wish you watery eyes with every smile . . .

"Long Black Eyelashes"

Long black eyelashes
squint around the eyes
Upper lip pursed

Selects every word very carefully
not one wasted
Always clear
Very precise

Saunters in a chair
as she speaks

Every word
Every sentence
Every thought
a sensual experience
Left hand waves
as if punctuation

Tiny
Petite

On every thought
she looks down

Is it nervous blinking?
nervous energy
Or flirtatious friendliness?

"A Conversation with You"

If the day was longer and the sun was hotter
It would all be bearable
With just ... A conversation with you
If my back hurt anymore and I
Slept any less than I already do
it would all be
bearable
With just ... A conversation with you
If the stress from life was harder
I could feel it through my body
And the fear of the unknown was on my back
It would be bearable
With just ... A conversation with you
The world looks so different
The world feels so different
The world is so different
With just ... A conversation with you.

"Little Black Dress"

Little black dress
Hugging those hips of hop
You sneak over those knees
Make me dream
Make me pop
Cream a little black secret shot
Little black dress
Wet and hot
You bounce
You rise
I rise
Its high rise
Bending
A peak that I so much seek
Perverted freak?
A man in heat?
Little black dress
You make my legs weak
Spread
Lift
Surprise
Let me try your body on for size
Use your legs as my belt
Harder than you have ever felt
In the front
On your side
Even from behind
Little black dress
I so Thank You for your time

"Beautiful Sleeper"

Beautiful sleeper
Eyes shut
firm
with lids that flicker with your erotic dreams
hands warm and soft
legs satin covered and curled
You hug the pillow as if I were near
moan a sigh that I wish I could hear
a toss
the quick turn
seeking warmth
hands slide between the thighs
Beautiful sleeper
shoulders taste of blossoms
your neck's aroma
like Lilies
you awake
as I slide my hands
under
your legs
around
your waist
I lift and cling
you smile and drift
you will
sleep a beautiful sleep
this morning
I watch as you dream
beautiful sleeper

"I Find Myself"

I wake to find myself wrapped
around your warm canvas body
as tight as the red on a Rose

I kiss your dark skin
taste the midnights sweat
and wipe away tears from your cheeks

I feel the shivers from your fears
tension in your neck
the panic of your stress

I grab you by the waist
and pull you closer

My sweat becomes yours
your fears become mine

The panic is soothed
and tears roll slower

I wake to find myself wrapped
around your warm canvas body
on this now very silent night

"Fantastic Profile"

Lids that blanket your eyes
like frost on a snowball
Close your lids and dream in
the poetics of this dream
of echoed voices
and weeping strings
As I watch a tear
push its way across
and down
the high cheekbones
higher that any woman deserves to have
I see your restless legs
cross and uncross and bounce

Your smile as pure as
the poetry
and that fantastic profile

"For Those Eyes Of Yours"

Not much time
for those eyes of yours
A brief encounter
mine to yours
I could not connect
with those eyes of yours
The dry air
The bumpy river
The sky bright
The Sun and heat

Not much time
for those eyes of yours
lilies, roses and baby's breath
surrounding us with life
A Saturday evening
meeting of chance
for those eyes of yours

Not much time
A brief encounter
mine to yours
I could not connect
for those eyes of yours

"Let Her Smoke in the Shower"

Let her smoke in the shower
with ashes
at her toes
panic drains her power

The water pounding
it thrusts on her back, neck and shoulders

Let her smoke in the shower

The knees are now weak
a sensation
rapture of wet smoke

A cloud hovers
over the curtain, rod and rings

Let her smoke in the shower

"She Sings Standards in the Corner"

clatter of ice
in glasses
whisper of top-shelf cocktails
kitchen's dinner specials
glide within this room
and across the bar
finds the singer in the corner
She sings standards
songs we all know
but seldom hear
She sits on a stool
dressed in a form-fitting sleeveless
sparkling-black dress
My Funny Valentine echoes from
her buffed-over lips
Her Carole Lombard locks
droop over her brow
and settle across her shoulders
She crosses her black-stocking legs
Bounces and smiles out
Sunny Side of the Street

The singer
sits in her corner
slips on her glasses
and hums out
Cry Me a River
patrons drink
some want to smoke but can't
The patrons clap
after each of her songs
Are they really listening?

They glance from their conversations
Is her voice the days-end elation
they don't know they need?

"So You Sit There ..."

So you sit there with the fully energized
smile that warms the outside wind chill
that hovers below freezing
Your movements are slow but then quick
So you sit there with the look of a Paris
cover girl
Long fingers dangle a butter knife over
the bread and hummus
So I sit here and look at the olive skin on
your toned and sculptured frame
Your hair pulled back
scarf droops
down your beautiful
neck line

So I sit there with hand on my tea and you
on your
coffee cup
My words are quick
sometimes mumbled
yours are like Spanglish silk

"That Place"

Take the wine and asparagus
that long black evening gown
the one that makes you wiggle
Pull your hair back
tight
Drink down that champagne
not wanting the cigarette
the habit that will give you the bad hostess breathe
Air kiss the cheeks of all your guest
some who you wish would be
in your warm bed at the end of this long evening
and a few you wish had never ended up there
Take your polite smile
polite laugh
Cover up that cattiness
in your mind
over the discovery of your best friends
winter ass
Take it
hold it in that dark place
That place
Take it
Until the evenings end

"Mislaid"

The thought of you not being here this evening
is a relief
I now feel the lack of hyperventilation
I don't have to see that perfect smile and hair meant
for
the goddess Isis or an angel
But then you enter
stage right
just like the actress you are
always on queue
you stride across the lobby
a dress from Macy's "only sexy department"
slit up the side
high enough to see that dangerous thigh
Oh, how nasty of you to tease me this way
I feel the sweat not only on my forehead but rolling
down my back
A shameful act on your part
Tease a man into
infatuations
You flick your hair back
why not just kick me in the groin
put it out of its misery

You smile my way and turn me into a thirteen-year-old
... again
I didn't like it the first time
why would I want to go back there?
I follow your perfume to my dangerous mind
you lead me to thoughts of babbling and dizziness
You are a cruel and hazardous angel
Why must you stroll across my path?

with movements of a spirit that comes from glossy
pages
When you finally disappear I find myself nowhere to be
found
How can someone
who I don't even know
make me feel so

Mislaid?

"Little Smile"

You gave me one day and the gift of your smile
It's amazing
how a little smile
could
be such a remembrance
Just add perfume
those legs
heat from your laughter
... and the gift of your smile

And now little smile
you elude me
Turn me
away
down
Make me chase without the confidence
of ever feeling the warmth
of that beautiful skin
of that cautious walk
or the gift
of kissing that little smile

"Lunch with Carole Lombard"

If I die today
I'd like to have lunch
with Carole Lombard

Hair platinum
Marbled eyes of blue
Vulgar sparks shouting from
lips of sensual innocence

The rapture of passion
With every move of her shoulders
every flick of her hair

Lunch every day
With Carole Lombard

"Wish I Could Have Tasted Your Lips"

If I tasted your lips they would be
Chocolate
Rich, Sweet
Creamy
Leaving me
wanting
all night
Sucking me
in like pudding
Your lips
Silky as your
Voice
Skin
as our
tongues
make love
I wish I could have tasted your lips

"The Woman with the Stunning Smile"

A woman who's lips look
as if they taste of sweet Christmas candy and wine
on a cool Autumn evening
Skin like a beautiful chocolate sundae
on a searing Summer night
with thoughts of its taste across my fingertips
The woman with the stunning smile
almost too beautiful to touch
A woman who deserves hugs
and magic kisses
Spring dandelions
and midnight wishes

The woman with the stunning smile

The Prose I write late at night...

"Why Does She"

I hear her voice and wonder why she lets me in
why she reads words so beautiful
and to me
why does the angel with a sensual voice
recite to me her expressions
why does she make me feel so inside her?
touch her warmth
and distant feelings
why does this woman
who comes in and out of my week
read poetry
such beautiful poetry
and with such swiftness of words
why does she not know how special she is as a woman
and a person?
why does she think she needs to be somewhere else in
life?
when life needs her here not over there
This woman with words so keen
so brilliant of choice
needs to take that step back
understand
that today
now
is the place
She has come to that home in life
where she has grown into one of her own lovely poems
a beautiful poem she wrote late one night
alone
sitting crossed legged
on her bed
She sees life more clear than most

expresses it with a simplicity that is so uncommon
but she still remains uncomfortable

Perhaps her next poem should be titled

"I am an exceptional woman"

with the sequel poem of

"... and beautiful, too"

"Your stunning smile and beautiful heart made me try to get to know you but to you I've become just an uncaring game and the frown you have given me and the disillusionment I now feel makes me try no longer..."

"The Pleasant and Savory Aroma of a Beautiful Woman and her Perfume ... Poetry, Cigarettes and Coffee ... A Paris Cafe' only in Black and White ..."

"And this is the point ..."

And this is the point in our life where we look back and see what we may not want to see
I can see the happiness but also the sadness I've caused and the stress under my eyes and the color of my hair has changed and the wrinkles on the back of my hands can be seen
And this is the point in our life where we know how many good years we may have left and how quickly the last years have gone and how we have wasted so much time on the past we cannot change and a future we cannot predict
Love is no guarantee of forever
Health will age
The touch of a leaf is beautiful at fifty but may mean nothing as a child
What's important at twelve is insignificant at forty
Rain on my face now is like silk but at ten it was just cold and wet
And this is the point in our life where we sometimes sleep more so we can dream of what was and then sleep less to cry over those we have loss and wish we still had and those we still have
Our three minutes of fame may never come
I'd settled for peace of mind
A sunny autumn day where the wind kisses my face with its breeze
Laughter instead of crying
A day with no worry
An hour of pure happiness
And this is the point in our life where falling comes so much easier and getting back up can be so much tougher but we refuse to stay down because giving up

is not an option we're used to and refuse to acknowledge

Forty years ago snow was a party and today it's a back ache

A hot day used to mean a beach but now it means a marina

I used to drink to fit in and now I couldn't care any less what "they' think

I can still out work many but my body will always yell at me for it later

My fears are for others

Life gets fragile

Those we love do too

We go on

And this is the point in our life where we look back ... we think ... it wasn't all good and wasn't all bad ... but this is a point in our life ...

"Tears"

He reaches for his loneliness
puts tears in his pockets
to escape

"Wish"

You sometimes wish you were in another skin
the skin that makes you uninhibited
the skin that makes you not so terrified of life
I frequently wish the same
I wish that the daily worries of life did not exist
that the night sweats and the day panics didn't happen
I wish today were tomorrow and then tomorrow
I will always wish were yesterday
Wishing is just so expected
Upon a star
for a dream
We all can afford to wish
I wish I had more to say

"This Is Love ... That Isn't"

So what if you didn't get that
You still have this
Do you really need that?
And that?
That's something else you didn't get
But this is still right in front of you
never left
It's always been there
Sometimes we are so busy trying to get that
we forget how important this is
Why is that so important?
especially when we don't even know what that really is
Can that hug you at night?
Can that make you feel warm?
This can
This can make you get goose bumps where that could
never find
I thought I wanted that
Don't we all?
We all have those moments where our minds stray
That seems so thrilling
That is so different
This is the same old thing
Or is it?
Maybe this seems the same because it refuses to
compromise
Like that?
I need this
I finally now know
I need this
If I could only hold onto this for a little bit longer
Maybe I could appreciate this more?

That comes and goes
This
Well, this is here for forever
This will be there when needed
And even when we don't want it
Never forget how important this is
Love isn't that
That isn't love
This is
This is love
And
isn't
this
just great

"Sometimes In the Winter"

Sometimes in the winter I go to our bench with some hot coffee and light a cigar and as I look up I can feel the snowflakes hitting my face and I imagine them being your cold snowy lips touching me

Sometimes in the winter I can sit on that bench just sipping the hot coffee and the steam from the coffee dances around my face like your hands on my cheeks

Sometimes in the winter I sit on that bench and when a gust of wind comes I can be hit with the most fantastic aroma of an over powering blast of your perfume ... and there are no flowers in sight

Sometimes in the winter I just sit on that bench and after a few minutes of missing you, I find peace

About the Author

Mark C. LLoyd is a published Poet and a produced Playwright who resides in Lockport, New York.

As a playwright, Director, board member and production consultant he has worked with many theater companies in the Buffalo, New York area.

To date he has directed over two dozen of his own one-act plays locally.

In 2009 Mark won an award for Directing from the Theatre Association of New York State and in May of 2006 he won for Writing "Hollywood Dreams-A Monologue".

He has been the featured reader and host at numerous Poetry events and has self-produced several artistic and theater productions.

His self-published Poetry chap-book from 2010 "Warm Blooded Mornings" is still available for sale as well as his 2012 miniature book "It's The Place You'll Find Me" by Destitute Press.

Presently Mark is working on editing another book of Poetry and two books of Plays as well as writing and directing a few independent movie projects.

And finally ...
for Boo-Boo

"You Were Not A Lion"

Did you really think you were a Lion?
A ferocious Tiger?
Didn't you know you were just a little furry runt?
A spoiled beautiful baby girl?
You didn't know you weren't the queen of the jungle?
Just my little spoiled queen
The only one you ever scared and controlled was me
It's called unconditional love ...
You had mine
Even if you were just a spoiled beautiful runt